THE PREVAILING POWER IN THE BLOOD OF JESUS

*And they overcame him by the blood of the Lamb,
and by the word of their testimony;
and they loved not their lives unto the death.*

Revelation 12:11

by
Franklin N. Abazie

The Prevailing Power in the Blood of Jesus
COPYRIGHT 2016 BY Franklin N Abazie
ISBN: 978-1-94513307-7

All right reserved. This book or any portion thereof may not be reproduced or used in any manner whatsoever without the express written permission of the publisher, except for the use of brief quotations in a book review. All Bible quotes are from King James Version and others as noted.

Published by: F N ABAZIE PUBLISHING HOUSE—aka, Empowerment Bookstore

That I may publish with the voice of thanksgiving and tell of all thy wondrous works.
Psalms 26:7

To order additional copies, wholesales or booking call:
the Church office (973-372-7518)
or Empowerment Bookstore Hotline (973-393-8518)

Worship address:
343 Sanford Avenue, Newark, New Jersey 07106
Administrative Head Office address:
33 Schley Street Newark New Jersey 07112
Email: pastorfranknto@yahoo.com
Website www.fnabaziehealingministries.org
Publishing House: www.fnabaziepublishinghouse.org

This book is a production of F N Abazie Publishing House. A publication Arms of Miracle of God Ministries 2016.
First Edition

CONTENTS

THE MANDATE OF THE COMMISSION......................iv
ARMS OF THE COMMISSION..v
INTRODUCTION..vi
CHAPTER 1
The Blood of Jesus..1
CHAPTER 2
The Mystery of the Blood of Jesus............................19
CHAPTER 3
The Benefits of the Blood of Jesus............................35
CHAPTER 4
Prayer of Salvation..59
CHAPTER 5
About the Author..66

THE MANDATE OF THE COMMISSION

"The moment is due to impact your world through the revival of the healing & miracle ministry of Jesus Christ of Nazareth.

"I am sending you to restore health unto thee and I will heal thee of thy wounds, said the Lord of Host."

ARMS OF THE COMMISSION

1) F N Abazie Ministries—Miracle of God Ministries (Miracle Chapel Intl)

2) F N Abazie TV Ministries: Global Television Ministry Outreach

3) F N Abazie Radio Ministries: Radio Broadcasting Outreach

4) F N Abazie Publishing House: Book Publication

5) F N Abazie Bible School: also called Word of Healing Bible School (W.O.H.B.S.)

6) F N Abazie Evangelistic Ass: Miracle of God Ministries: Global Crusade

7) Empowerment Bookstore: Book distribution

8) F N Abazie Helping Hands: Meeting the Help of the Needy Worldwide

9) F N Abazie Disaster Recovery Mission: Global Disaster Recovery

10) F N Abazie Prison Ministry: Prison Ministry For All Convicts "Second Chance"

Some of our ministry arms are awaiting the appointed time to commence.

INTRODUCTION

Over my few years in the gospel ministry, I have heard a lot of church folks plead the blood of Jesus Christ—especially in prayer. I believe there is a prevailing mystery concerning the blood of Jesus Christ. Among the potent power in the blood of Jesus Christ is the prevailing power in the blood of Jesus Christ.

THE BLOOD OF JESUS, I believe, is among the strongest forces of the SPIRIT. As a SPIRITUAL LAW enforcement officer with the accreditation of the SPIRIT and a WARRANT for the ARREST OF THE DEVIL, we are obligated to enforce the laws of the spirit with our last weapon—THE BLOOD OF JESUS CHRIST, appropriately.

A lot of church people have misinterpreted and misrepresented the mystery of the blood of Jesus Christ.

"And almost all things are by the law purged with blood; and without shedding of blood is no remission." (Hebrews 9:22)

The blood of Jesus Christ is our shield of **protection** over all the wiles and schemes of the devil. *"And when I see the blood, I will pass over you, and the plague shall not be upon you to destroy you, when I smite the land of Egypt."* (Exodus 12:13)

The blood of Jesus Christ is our medium for true confession. *"But if we walk in the light, as he is in the light, we have fellowship one with another, and the blood of Jesus Christ his Son cleanseth us from all sin."* (1 John 1:7)

"How much more shall the blood of Christ, who through the eternal Spirit offered himself without spot to God, purge your conscience from dead works to serve the living God." (Hebrews 9:14)

Although we live in a very challenging time, in my opinion the blood of Jesus Christ is our last weapon to pull the trigger against the devil. *"And they overcame him by the blood of the Lamb, and by the word of their testimony; and they loved not their lives unto the death."* (Revelation 12:11)

In this publication, you will appreciate and embrace the teaching which the Holy Spirit will be revealing in this book. Truly, there is an overwhelming POWER IN THE BLOOD OF JESUS CHRIST. It is that PREVAILING DIMENSION of THE BLOOD OF JESUS CHRIST that I will be bringing to light, with the help of God, Be blessed as you read.

HAPPY READING!

"And they overcame him by the blood of the Lamb, and by the word of their testimony."
Revelation 12:11

HIGHLIGHTS

QUALIFICATIONS TO PLEAD THE BLOOD OF JESUS

REPENTANCE

The blood of Jesus will not prevail for us, as long as there is sin in our lives. Especially the sin that easily besets us. Only dogs return to their vomits. Iniquity means the repeating of sin over and over again. Every time we repeat a particular sin, we are swallowing our own vomit.

If we must plead THE BLOOD OF JESUS CHRIST and get instant results, we must be ready for genuine **repentance**. *"But if we walk in the light, as he is in the light, we have fellowship one with another, and the blood of Jesus Christ his Son cleanseth us from all sin. If we say that we have no sin, we deceive ourselves, and the truth is not in us. If we confess our sins, he is faithful and just to forgive us our sins, and to cleanse us from all unrighteousness. If we say that we have not sinned, we make him a liar, and his word is not in us."* (1 John 1:7-10)

Although the first step into **healing** is **repentance**, it is also the qualification step to **plead the blood of Jesus Christ**. The HOLY SPIRIT intervention is quick and swift only when God sees a humble, **repented heart**. Peter replied to a question from the crowd of "what shall we do?" with: *"Repent and be baptized every one of you, in the name of Jesus Christ for the* *forgiveness of your sins. And you will receive the gift of the Holy Spirit."* (Acts 2:38) Every time we truly REPENT, GOD genuinely RESTORES OUR LIVES. *"Therefore say thou unto them, Thus saith the Lord of hosts; Turn ye unto me, saith the Lord of hosts, and I will turn unto you, saith the Lord of hosts."* (Zechariah 1:3)

FAITH

But without faith it is impossible to please him: for he that cometh to God must believe that he is, and that he is a rewarder of them that diligently seek him.
Hebrews 11:6

THE MYSTERY OF THE BLOOD OF JESUS is not fully activated when we lack FAITH. We are admonished in the scriptures: *"But without faith it is impossible to please him: for he that cometh to God must believe that he is, and that he is a rewarder of them that diligently seek him."* (Hebrews 11:6) If we must plead the blood of Jesus Christ and get genuine results, **we must have faith in God.** *"And Jesus answering saith unto them, Have faith in God."* (Mark 11:22)

DECISION

If we must PLEAD the blood of Jesus, we must come into agreement with THE HOLY SPIRIT. We must decide on making eternity with Jesus Christ—salvation. Unless we **repent** and **accept** Jesus Christ as our Lord and savior, we are not ready to receive the Holy Spirit. Decisions are the pillars to determine the outcome of our lives. Most of the events of our lifetime were all directly proportional to our decisions. Decisions are the building blocks into the success of our future.

For example, whenever we settle for a less paying job, we are entitled to the lower wages and lower salaries. Lazarus settled to eat crumbs. *"And there was a certain beggar named Lazarus, which was laid at his gate, full of sores, And desiring to be fed with the crumbs which fell from the rich man's table: moreover the dogs came and licked his sores."* (Luke 16:20-21) Despite all the wealth of the father, the prodigal son decided to eat the pig's food.

THE DECISION OF THE PRODIGAL SON

And he said, A certain man had two sons: And the younger of them said to his father, Father, give me the portion of goods that falleth to me. And he divided unto them his living. And not many days after the younger son gathered all together, and took his journey into a far country, and there wasted his substance with riotous living. And when he had spent all, there arose a mighty famine in that land; and he began to be in want. And he went and joined himself to a citizen of that country; and he sent him into his fields to feed swine. And he would fain have filled his belly with the husks that the swine did eat: and no man gave unto him. And when he came to himself, he said, How many hired servants of my father's have bread enough and to spare, and I perish with hunger! I will arise and go to my father, and will say unto him, Father, I have sinned against heaven, and before thee, And am no more worthy to be called thy son: make me as one of thy hired servants. And he arose, and came to his father. But when he was yet a great way off, his father saw him, and had compassion, and ran, and fell on his neck, and kissed him. And the son said unto him, Father, I have sinned against heaven, and in thy sight, and am no more worthy to be called thy son. But the father said to his servants, Bring forth the best robe, and put it on him; and put a ring on his hand, and shoes on his feet: And bring hither the fatted calf, and kill it; and let us eat, and be merry: For this my son was dead, and is alive again; he was lost, and is found. And they began to be merry.

Luke 15:14-24

PRAYER

But ye beloved, building up your selves on your most holy faith, praying in the Holy Ghost.
Jude 1:20

Whenever we are praying in the spirit, we must appropriate **the blood of Jesus accurately and precisely**. The **blood of Jesus Christ** is our **access code** into the **realms of the spirit. Our prayer** is not complete especially until we **pray in the language of the angels** by praying in tongue and **pleading the blood of Jesus Christ**.

A FEW HIGH POINTS

1) We must pray from a genuine repented heart.

2) We must pray with a pure conscience.

3) We must pray kingdom prayers—thy kingdom come."

4) We must pray for one another.

5) We must pray with love.

6) We must pray sincerely.

7) We must pray for the promotion of the kingdom of God.

8) We must pray for our pastor and elders in the church.

9) We must pray for our leaders.

10) We must pray for our families.

11) We must pray for the sick.

12) We must pray for the church of Christ.

PRAYER POINT TO PLEAD THE BLOOD OF CHRIST

And they overcame him by the blood of the Lamb, and by the Word of their testimony; as a weapon.
Revelation 12:11

1. Thank You, Father for the provision of the blood of Jesus.

2. I proclaim victory in my life by the blood of Jesus.

3. I plead the blood of Jesus to all my prevailing challenges in life.

4. I plead the blood of Jesus upon my body.

5. I soak my finances in the blood of Jesus.

6. I paralyze all satanic oppressors delegated against me by the blood of Jesus.

7. I plead the blood of Jesus over finances, in the name of Jesus.

8. By the blood of Jesus, I stand against all device of the devil against me.

9. I stand upon the Word of God and I declare myself unmovable, in the name of Jesus.

10. Let every door that I have opened to the enemy be closed forever with the blood of Jesus.

11. Make each of the following powerful confessions 70 times:

—Through the blood of Jesus, I have been redeemed out of the hands of the devil.

—I walk in the light and the blood of Jesus cleanses me from all sins.

—Through the blood of Jesus, I have the life of God in me.

—Through the blood of Jesus, I have access to the presence of the Lord.

12. I paralyze and cut off the head of Goliath with the blood of Jesus.

13. If there is anything in me that is not of God, I don't want it. Depart, in the mighty name of Jesus.

14. Let the blood of the cross stand between me and any dark power delegated against me.

15. I curse every work of darkness in my life to dry to the roots by the blood of Jesus.

16. I overcome, paralyze and strip naked—spirit of demotion, financial downgrading—by the blood of Jesus

17. Let the power of the blood of Jesus be released on my behalf and let it speak against every dead bone in my life.

18. Let the power of the blood of Jesus be released on my behalf and let it speak against every stubborn mountain in my life.

19. In the name of Jesus, I plead the blood of Jesus.

20. In the name of Jesus, I apply the blood of Jesus over my house.

21. In the name of Jesus, I soak myself in the blood of Jesus.

22. In the name of Jesus, I apply the blood of Jesus. Demons, you cannot re-enter my house.

23. I draw a circle of the blood of Jesus around me.

24. I draw the blood line of protection around my property.

25. I overcome you Satan, by the blood of the Lamb.

26. You cannot put any sickness on me because I am redeemed by the blood of the Lamb.

27. Let the blood of Jesus speak confusion into the camp of the enemy.

28. Let the blood of Jesus speak destruction unto every evil growth in my life.

29. Let the blood of Jesus speak disappearance unto every infirmity in my life.

30. Let the blood of Jesus restore every broken marriage.

31. Let the blood of Jesus help my infirmities.

32. I sprinkle the blood of Jesus on all my income.

33. Let the blood of Jesus over every frustrating issue in my life right now..

34. You evil power, I paralyze you by the power of the blood of Jesus.

35. I destroyed by the blood every evil power militating against my life.

36. I plead the blood against every evil force militating against my ministry.

37. Let the blood of Jesus minister victory against every evil work in my life.

38. Let the blood of Jesus destroy any evil plantation in my life.

39. I minister death unto the enemy of progress in my life by the blood of Jesus.

40. I bind the staying power of any problem by the blood of Jesus.

41. I create a boundary against you, devil, by the blood of Jesus.

42. I plead the blood of Jesus against any marine forces working against my life.

43. I enter the Holy of Holies by the blood of Jesus.

44. I plead the blood of Jesus against the spirit of stag-

nation in my life.

45. I plead the blood of Jesus against the delay of my miracles.

46. I plead the blood of Jesus against frustration at the sight of success.

47. I plead the blood of against the lack of divine comforters.

48. I plead the blood of Jesus against fruitless efforts in my life.

49. I plead the blood of Jesus against anyone occupying my position.

50. I plead the blood of Jesus against every delayed and denied promotion.

51. I plead the blood of Jesus against dead accounts.

52. I plead the blood of Jesus against false accusation in my life.

53. I plead the blood of Jesus against lost opportunities in my life.

54. I plead the blood of Jesus against all negative prophecies.

55. I plead the blood of Jesus against confusion spirits.

56. I plead the blood of Jesus against hardship.

CHAPTER 1
THE BLOOD OF JESUS

And they overcame him by the blood of the Lamb, and by the word of their testimony; and they loved not their lives unto the death.
Revelation 12:11

WHAT IS IN THE BLOOD?

The blood of Jesus is the last weapon to pull the trigger against the devil and is a force of the **Spirit** —the three that bear record must agree. The **Spirit** and the **water** and the **blood**—these three agree in one. *"And there are three that bear witness in earth, the Spirit, and the water, and the blood: and these three agree in one."* (1 John 5:8)

The life of the flesh is in the **blood of Jesus Christ**.

For the life of the flesh is in the blood.
Leviticus 17:11

WHAT IS IN THE BLOOD?

The spirit, the water and the blood are all the components of the blood of Jesus. Let's briefly examine these characteristics of these components.

THE SPIRIT

The spirit of jesus is the overcoming **force** to **dominate the devil cheaply.** *"But if the Spirit of him that raised up Jesus from the dead dwell in you, he that raised up Christ from the dead shall also quicken your mortal bodies by his Spirit that dwelleth in you."* (Romans 8:11)

Remember...

It is the SPIRIT OF GOD that bears witness. *"The Spirit itself beareth witness with our spirit, that we are the children of God."* (Romans 8:16) The SPIRIT always bears witness for us—especially when we plead the blood of Jesus Christ.

WATER

WATER is a symbol of the Holy Spirit. The same way water is used naturally to quench thirst and to wash off dirts, that's the same way water is **deployed** in the **realms of the spirit**. *"That he might sanctify and cleanse it with the washing of water by the word."* (Ephesians 5:26) *"For I will pour water upon him that is thirsty, and floods upon the dry ground: I will pour my spirit upon thy seed, and my blessing upon thine offspring."* (Isaiah 44:3)

THE BLOOD

And they overcame him by the blood of the Lamb,
and by the word of their testimony;
and they loved not their lives unto the death.
Revelation 12:11

This is he that came by water and blood,
even Jesus Christ; not by water only,
but by water and blood. And it is the Spirit
that beareth witness, because the Spirit is truth.
For there are three that bear record in heaven,
the Father, the Word, and the Holy Ghost: and these
three are one. And there are three that bear witness
in earth, the Spirit, and the water, and the blood: and
these three agree in one.
1 John 5:6-8

HOW DO I PLEAD THE BLOOD OF JESUS?

We must plead the blood of Jesus loudly with our mouths. We must do it repeatedly and enforce it strongly against the kingdom of darkness and Satan's cohorts.

HOW DO I PRAY?

We must humble ourselves in **prayer** with **attention, reverence and respect** to God.

WE MUST HUMBLE OUR SELVES IRRESPECTIVE OF OUR AFFLUENCE IN THE SOCIETY OR JOB POSITION

If my people, which are called by my name, shall humble themselves, and pray, and seek my face, and turn from their wicked ways; then will I hear from heaven, and will forgive their sin, and will heal their land. Now mine eyes shall be open, and mine ears attent unto the prayer that is made in this place.
2 Chronicles 7:14-15

WE MUST RESPECT & HONOR THE PRESENCE OF THE ALMIGHTY GOD

Every time we despise the presence of God, we suffer the consequence. *"For them that honour me I will honour, and they that despise me shall be lightly esteemed."* (1 Samuel 2:30)

We are commanded by the scripture to **honor God**. If we are obedient to our earthly parents, how much more our **heavenly father**? *"Honour thy father and mother; which is the first commandment with promise."* (Ephesians 6:2)

We prove our son ship when we **honor God in**

prayers. *"A son honoureth his father, and a servant his master: if then I be a father, where is mine honour? and if I be a master, where is my fear? saith the Lord of hosts unto you, O priests, that despise my name. And ye say, Wherein have we despised thy name?"* (Malachi 1:6-9)

WE MUST REVERENCE GOD IN PRAYERS

Prayer is a two-way communication between us and God. **Prayer** means talking and listening directly to God with reverence, respect, attention and love. Although so many of us are selfish, we just want God to **hear us out**. We don't want to LISTEN TO GOD talk back to us. Prayer is a two-way communication channel. Whenever we speak to God in **prayer**, we must create time to **mediate**, and **listen** when God is talking back to us **with respect, love, humility and revrence**. We must **reverence** the name of God in **prayers** because it is *holy. "He sent redemption unto his people: he hath commanded his covenant forever: holy and reverend is his name."* (Psalms 111:9)

Although we must **respect, reverence and humble ourselves** before God, if our heart is not right with Him, He will not hear us. *"Then shall they cry unto the Lord, but he will not hear them: he will even hide his face from them at that time, as they have behaved themselves ill in their doings."* (Micah 3:4)

As long as we live in sin and in disobedience,

God will not hear our prayers. *"But your iniquities have separated between you and your God, and your sins have hid his face from you, that he will not hear."* (Isaiah 59:2) *"Therefore it is come to pass, that as he cried, and they would not hear; so they cried, and I would not hear, saith the Lord of hosts."* (Zechariah 7:13) Prayers must be done **correctly** for it to **receive speedy intervention**.

WHAT IS THE RIGHT WAY TO PRAY UNTO GOD?

Our typical example on how to **pray** is the prayer Jesus taught his disciples to pray in Luke.

*And it came to pass, that, as he was praying
in a certain place, when he ceased,
one of his disciples said unto him,
Lord, teach us to pray, as John also taught his disciples.
And he said unto them, When ye pray, say,
Our Father which art in heaven, Hallowed be thy name.
Thy kingdom come. Thy will be done, as in heaven,
so in earth. Give us day by day our daily bread.
And forgive us our sins; for we also forgive every one
that is indebted to us. And lead us not into temptation;
but deliver us from evil.*
Luke 11:1-4

RESPECT
…say, Our Father which art in heaven…

REVERENCE
...Hallowed be thy name. Thy kingdom come...

HONOR
...Thy will be done, as in heaven, so in earth...

REQUEST
...Give us day by day our daily bread. And forgive us our sins; for we also forgive every one that is indebted to us. And lead us not into temptation; but deliver us from evil.

The Holy Scripture attested that God does not hear sinners, but if any man worships Him, and does His will, **God** is covenantly **obligated to intervene.** *"Now we know that God heareth not sinners: but if any man be a worshipper of God, and doeth his will, him he heareth."* (John 9:31)

WHO IS A SINNER

Everyone operating outside of the commandment of the scripture is a sinner, in my opinion. Whenever you disobey God, reject God, mock God, ignorantly neglect the presence and sovereignty of God, you are a sinner. *"He that committeth sin is of the devil; for the devil sinneth from the beginning;For this purpose the son of God was manifested that he might destroy the works of the devil."* (1 John 3:8)

It is easy to lie and hide from a man, but very difficult to hide from the **presence of God**. For God does not look like man. *"For my thoughts are not your thoughts, neither are your ways my ways, saith the Lord. For as the heavens are higher than the earth, so are my ways higher than your ways, and my thoughts than your thoughts."* (Isaiah 55:8-9)

For the Lord seeth not as man seeth; for man looketh on the outward appearance, but the Lord looketh on the heart."
1 Samuel 16:9

Remember...
David could not run away from **the presence of God**. David said: *"Whither shall I go from thy spirit? or whither shall I flee from thy presence? If I ascend up into heaven, thou art there: if I make my bed in hell, behold, thou art there. If I take the wings of the morning, and dwell in the uttermost parts of the sea; Even there shall thy hand lead me, and thy right hand shall hold me."* (Psalms 139:7-10)

He that covereth his sins shall not prosper: but whoso confesseth and forsaketh them shall have mercy.
Proverbs 28:13

We live in a time where there is so much **sinful** advertisement hitting us at every street corner, from the newspapers to the television, we are bombarded daily with immoral images—**alcohol** ads and **sinful lust** appeal to us from the TV. As simple as sin can be interpreted, it is extremely difficult for church folks to differentiate between what is **sinful** from what is **righteous**. *"He that doeth righteousness is righteous, even as he is righteous."* (1 John 3:7)

WHO IS A SINNER?

Unless otherwise stated, all who live in disobedience of the commandment of God can be called **sinners**. Everyone living an unethical, unrighteous and immoral lifestyle is a sinner. We are admonished to *"love not the world, neither the things that are in the world. If any man love the world, the love of the Father is not in him. For all that is in the world, the lust of the flesh, and the lust of the eyes, and the pride of life, is not of the Father, but is of the world."* (1 John 2:15-16)

James also had a profound statement about sin:

From whence come wars and fightings among you? come they not hence, even of your lusts that war in your members? Ye lust, and have not: ye kill, and desire to have, and cannot obtain: ye fight and war, yet ye have not, because ye ask not. Ye ask, and receive not, because ye ask amiss, that ye may consume it upon your lusts. Ye adulterers and adulteresses, know ye not that the friendship of the world is enmity with God? whosoever therefore will be a friend of the world is the enemy of God. Do ye think that the scripture saith in vain, The spirit that dwelleth in us lusteth to envy?"
James 4:1-5

*Examine yourselves, whether ye be in the faith;
prove your own selves. Know ye not your own selves,
how that Jesus Christ is in you, except ye be reprobates?*
2 Corinthians 13:5

The Holy Bible defined **sin** from **righteousness** in a clear and precise term that cannot be mistaken. Despite our **ignorance**, some of us still **misrepresent and misinterpret** the scripture. We tend to **justify our sinful actions** with our own **interpretation** of the scripture. From my own small understanding, everyone operating within the scope of Galatians 5:20-21 is classified as a sinner.

Now the works of the flesh are manifest, which are these; Adultery, fornication, uncleanness, lasciviousness, idolatry, witchcraft, hatred, variance, emulations, wrath, strife, seditions, heresies, envyings, murders, drunkenness, revellings, and such like: of the which I tell you before, as I have also told you in time past, that they which do such things shall not inherit the kingdom of God.
Galatians 5:20-21

Further supporting scripture...

*But the fearful, and unbelieving, and the abominable, and murderers, and whoremongers, and sorcerers, and idolaters, and all liars, shall have their part in the lake which burneth with fire and brimstone:
which is the second death.*
Revelation 21:8

WHO, THEREFORE, IS A SINNER?

1) The Lazy Man: There are a lot of church folks who uses **prayer and fasting** as excuses why they should not do productive work. It is sinful for any able-bodied man or woman to fold their hands and make themselves beggars before man and the Spirit of God. The Bible says, *"the sluggard will not plow by reason of the cold; therefore shall he beg in harvest, and have nothing."* (Proverbs 20:4)

In my own understanding, laziness is a sin. *"For even when we were with you, this we commanded you, that if any would not work, neither should he eat."* (2 Thessalonians 3:10)

Covenant mentality demands that we all understand that God has done His part over our lives. Jesus said I must work. It is dignified for every believer to earn money through the work of their hands—*"The sleep of a labouring man is sweet, whether he eat little or much."* (Ecclesiastes 5:12)

Although most lazy people live in denial and tend to blame someone else, nevertheless, Godliness demands that we take absolute responsibility for the outcome of our lives.

2) Unbelievers: In my view, all that have not acknowledged Jesus Christ as Lord and savior are sinners. The Bible says *God heareth not sinners*. Without contradiction, all unbelievers live in a sinful lifestyle. Unless God has mercy, most unbelievers will not make eternity in heaven.

HOW DO I COME OUT OF SIN?

These prevailing, dominating, controlling forces will not casually go away. Unless you're taking actions by faith, those evil forces will continue to remote control your life and destiny.

You must *REPENT*, *CONFESS* and *PROCLAIM* the **LORD JESUS CHRIST.**

The word says as many as received him, to them gave He power to become the sons of God. Even to them that believe on his name.

To qualify for divine visitation, do the following (with sincerity):

1) *Acknowledge* that you are a sinner and that He died for you. (Romans 3:23)

2) *Repent of your sins.* (Acts 3:19, Luke 13:5, 2 Peter 3:9)

3) *Believe in your heart* that Jesus died for your sin. (Romans 10:10)

4) *Confess Jesus as the Lord over your life.* (Romans 10:10, Acts 2:21)

Now repeat this Prayer after me—

Say Lord Jesus, I accept you today, as my Lord and my savior, forgive me of my sins wash me with your blood. Right now, I believe, I am sanctified, I am save, I am free,

*I am free from the Power of sin to serve the Lord Jesus.
Thank you Lord for saving me. Amen.*

Congratulations.

YOU ARE NOW A BORN AGAIN CHRISTIAN!

WHEN & HOW OFTEN SHOULD WE PRAY?

ALWAYS

Although there are never enough **prayers**, we are commanded by the Holy Bible to **pray always**. *"Praying always with all prayer and supplication in the Spirit, and watching thereunto with all perseverance and supplication for all saints."* (Ephesians 6:18)

*I thank my God upon every remembrance of you,
Always in every prayer of mine for you all making
request with joy.*
Philippians 1:3-4

We must **pray always**. *"We give thanks to God and the Father of our Lord Jesus Christ, praying always for you."* (Collosians 1:3)

Oftentimes, most of us **pray and backslide**. We are commanded to **pray without ceasing**. *"Pray without ceasing."* (1 Thessalonians 5:17) We miss our opportunity and our due season when we **pray and faint**. "And let us not be weary in well doing: for in due season we shall reap, if we faint not." (Galatians 6:9)

HOW SHOULD WE PRAY?

WE MUST PRAY IN THE SPIRIT

Satan does not understand the language of the **Spirit**. Every time we **pray in the spirit** we confuse and defeat the devil with the language of the angels. "For if I pray in an unknown tongue, my spirit prayeth, but my understanding is unfruitful. What is it then? I will pray with the spirit, and I will pray with the understanding also: I will sing with the spirit, and I will sing with the understanding also." (1 Corinthians 14:14-15)

WE MUST PRAY SINCERELY FROM A GENUINE CONSCIENCE

Remember Hanna, for example

"And she was in bitterness of soul, and prayed unto the Lord, and wept sore. And she vowed a vow, and said, O Lord of hosts, if thou wilt indeed look on the affliction of thine handmaid, and remember me, and not forget thine handmaid, but wilt give unto thine handmaid a man child, then I will give him unto the Lord all the days of his life, and there shall no razor come upon his head. And it came to pass, as she continued praying before the Lord, that Eli marked her mouth." (1 samuel 1:10-12)

Remember Hezekiah as a second example

"In those days was Hezekiah sick unto death. And Isaiah the prophet the son of Amoz came unto him, and said unto him, Thus saith the Lord, Set thine house in order: for thou shalt die, and not live. Then Hezekiah turned his face toward the wall, and prayed unto the Lord, And said, Remember now, O Lord, I beseech thee, how I have walked before thee in truth and with a perfect heart, and have done that which is good in thy sight. And Hezekiah wept sore." (Isaiah 38:1-3)

"Then Jonah prayed unto the Lord his God out of the fish's belly, And said, I cried by reason of mine affliction unto the Lord, and he heard me; out of the belly of hell cried I, and thou heardest my voice." (Jonah 2:1-2)

WE MUST PRAY FROM A THANKSGIVING, CHEERFUL HEART

If we must **pray** and get **rewarded**, we must enter into **His presence** with thanksgiving—not with **murmuring and complaining**. Never come to the place of prayer with anger, bitterness and sadness. *"Enter into his gates with thanksgiving, and into his courts with praise: be thankful unto him, and bless his name."* (Psalms 100:4)

WE MUST PRAY WITH FAITH

Like I stated earlier, the prayer of faith will not save the sick unless there is **faith in such prayer**. *"But* *let him ask in faith, with no doubting, for the one who doubts is like a wave of the sea that is driven and tossed by the wind."* (James 1:6)

What Should We Pray For

WE MUST PRAY KINGDOM ORIENTED PRAYERS

We shall never prevail in prayers unless we focus on the kingdom of God. *"But seek ye first the kingdom of God, and his righteousness; and all these things shall be added unto you."* (Matthew 6:33) *"And he said unto them, When ye pray, say, Our Father which art in heaven, Hallowed be thy name. Thy kingdom come. Thy will be done, as in heaven, so in earth."* (Luke 11:1-2)

One of my great mentors, Archbishop Benson Idahosa, used to say it this way: "Go after the commission in prayers and the commission will bring the addition in our lives."

SUMMARY OF CHAPTER ONE

Prayer is a two-way communication dialogue. It is a serene meeting place with God, where **divinity** meets with **humanity**. Dynamic prayers require that we understand the **right way to pray to God**.

And it came to pass, that, as he was praying in a certain place, when he ceased, one of his disciples said unto him, Lord, teach us to pray, as John also taught his disciples. And he said unto them, When ye pray, say, Our Father which art in heaven, Hallowed be thy name. Thy kingdom come. Thy will be done, as in heaven, so in earth. Give us day by day our daily bread. And forgive us our sins; for we also forgive every one that is indebted to us. And lead us not into temptation; but deliver us from evil.
Luke 11:1-4

WE MUST RESPECT GOD IN PRAYER
...say, Our Father which art in heaven...

WE MUST REVERENCE GOD IN PRAYER
...Hallowed be thy name. Thy kingdom come...

WE MUST HONOR GOD IN PRAYER
...Thy will be done, as in heaven, so in earth...

WE MUST MAKE OUR SUPPLICATION KNOWN TO GOD IN PRAYERS

...Give us day by day our daily bread. And forgive us our sins; for we also forgive every one that is indebted to us. And lead us not into temptation;
but deliver us from evil.

Remember...God does not hear sinners. *"Now we know that God heareth not sinners: but if any man be a worshipper of God, and doeth his will, him he heareth."* (John 9:31)

The keys to divine health are released by God on the platform of the power and dynamics of prayer.

I must tell you this and it must be here— *prayer works.* I am a living testimony of the handiwork of prayer. I admonish you, therefore, to begin a **prayer lifestyle**. The people that **pray** do not develop mental disease. The people that **pray** do not die untimely deaths. As long as you **pray,** there is help on the way.

Remember...

The potency and power of prayer is released on the platform of the covenant.

CHAPTER 2

THE MYSTERY OF THE BLOOD OF JESUS

Over the years, there's always been a prevailing argument concerning the blood of Jesus—simply because he knew no sin, but became sin for us all. *"And all things are of God, who hath reconciled us tohimself by Jesus Christ, and hath given to us the ministry of reconciliation; To wit, that God was in Christ, reconciling the world unto himself, not imputing their trespasses unto them; and hath committed unto us the word of reconciliation. Now then we are ambassadors for Christ, as though God did beseech you by us: we pray you in Christ's stead, be ye reconciled to God. For he hath made him to be sin for us, who knew no sin; that we might be made the righteousness of God in him."* (2 Corinthians 5:18-21)

THE BLOOD OF JESUS CHRIST IS QUICK AND POWERFUL

Who is he that overcometh the world, but he that believeth that Jesus is the Son of God? This is he that came by water and blood, even Jesus Christ; not by water only, but by water and blood. And it is the Spirit that beareth witness, because the Spirit is truth.For there are three that bear record in heaven, the Father, the Word, and the Holy Ghost: and these three are one. And there are three that bear witness in earth, the Spirit, and the water, and the blood: and these three agree in one.
1 John 5:5-8

Although the **blood of Jesus is our last weapon to pull the trigger against the devil**, it is also an instrument of **reconcilation and peace**. *"And, having made peace through the blood of his cross, by him to reconcile all things unto himself; by him, I say, whether they be things in earth, or things in heaven."* (Colossians 1:20)

The Bible says, *"For if the blood of bulls and of goats, and the ashes of an heifer sprinkling the unclean, sanctifieth to the purifying of the flesh: How much more shall the blood of Christ, who through the eternal Spirit offered himself without spot to God, purge your conscience from dead works to serve the living God?"* (Hebrews 9:13-14)

THE MYSTERY OF THE BLOOD OF JESUS

The blood of Jesus is a mystery because of a combination of these factors: prevailing power in the blood, dominating power in the blood, overcoming power in the blood of Jesus, conqering power in the blood of Jesus Christ and testimonial power in the blood of Jesus Christ.

Blotting out the handwriting of ordinances that was against us, which was contrary to us, and took it out of the way, nailing it to his cross; And having spoiled principalities and powers, he made a shew of them openly, triumphing over them in it.
Colossians 2:14-15

So many of us church folks talk so much about the blood of Jesus, but we fail to understand the mysteries that are in the blood of Jesus Christ. The blood of Jesus is the ransom that the Father **paid for our sins**. *"And almost all things are by the law purged with blood; and without shedding of blood is no remission."* (Hebrews 9:22)

We were **redeemed by the blood of Jesus Christ**. It is written, *"Christ hath redeemed us from the curse of the law, being made a curse for us: for it is written, Cursed is every one that hangeth on a tree: That the blessing of Abraham might come on the Gentiles through Jesus Christ; that we might receive the promise of the Spirit through faith."* (Galatians 3:13-14)

The blood of Jesus is inexplicable in its working power. The blood of Jesus is dynamic, quick and powerful—sharper than a two-edged sword. The above scripture summarized the purpose of the blood of Jesus in a nutshell. It is written: *"Purge out therefore the old leaven, that ye may be a new lump, as ye are unleavened. For even Christ our passover is sacrificed for us."* (1 Corinthians 5:7)

HIS DESTINY WAS THE CROSS....

HIS PURPOSE WAS LOVE....

HIS REASON WAS YOU....

*And they overcame him by the blood of the Lamb,
and by the word of their testimony;
and they loved not their lives unto the death.*
Revelation 12:11

HEALING KEYS

1) Always carry a positive mindset, regardless of the prevailing circumstances.

2) Always tell yourself the truth before you lie about it.

3) If the truth be told, you are a branch of His blessings, the planting of the Lord.

4) Never confess that you are sick to the hearing of the member of your body.

5) Positive confession with faith yields positive results.

6) Every cures of man have no power to prevail over your life.

7) A merry heart is medicinal and health to your body.

8) Spiritual and emotional well-being is vital to happiness in life.

9) To avoid depression, never have regrets.

10) Never be anxious in life to avoid anxiety.

11) Always live today for today to be at peace with your spirit and with God.

11) You're unique because your challenges are tailored to you only.

12) The blessing always dominates the curses any day.

13) Decisions are the wheels of life.

14) We either ride into fame or into shame.

15) Daily exercise and some reading of the Bible gurantees good health.

16) Every day is God's day. No day created by God is a disapointment.

17) Stay away from sweet stuff—they are temporary.

18) Sugar is sweet to your taste, beware! It also contributes to diabetes.

19) A good prayer life gurantees longivity.

20) People that pray in tongues do not develop mental disease.

21) Always be positive in everything.

22) Always have a mentor in life that will oppose and fight the tormentor.

23) Always have someone in life to learn from.

24) Tell everybody what you plan to do and someone will help you do it.

25) Winners fight to the last.

26) Quitters never win in life.

27) Soul winners are heirs to the kingdom of god.

28) Soul winners never lack help.

29) Soul winners are cerified with divine help.

30) God is always looking for soul winners to bless.

31) Life is a warfare and not a funfare.

32) In life you fight for all you possess.

33) No man or woman was born rich.

34) In your lifetime do something positive to impact your world.

35) Take care of your life today—you don't have one to spare.

36) Take your life serious before the devil take you down.

37) Always be cheerful at all times.

38) Regardless of the prevailing circumstances around you, your life is in the hand of God.

39) God is the super surgeon that will spiritually-surgically heal you.

40) Always expect help from above and not from abroad.

41) Man will disappoint you, but god will appoint you.

42) The joy of the lord is always our strength.

43) Spiritual height is not measured in length or breath.

44) If you go deeper with God, you will see deeper.

45) Your next level in life is full of recognition.

46) Go to where you are celebrated and not where you are tolerated.

47) Develop yourself in the area of your calling in life.

48) A lifestyle of thanks given keeps God 24/7 on duty on our behalf.

49) Develop a lifestyle of thanksgiving.

50) Thanksgiving guarantees our access to obtain the promises.

DECISION KEYS

1) Nothing changes until you make up your mind.

2) Decision is the gateway to deliverance.

3) Until you decide, no one will decide for you.

4) Your prosperity is proportional to your decisions.

5) The decision you make will determine the future you will create

6) Decision creates future and fulfills destinies.

7) Decision beautifies our future.

8) Decision keeps you out of trouble.

9) Decision exempts you from evil.

10) Decision gurantees eternity.

11) You can only go far in life by your faith decisions.

12) You are poor because you made such decisions

13) Make a decision and change your life.

14) Life changing decisions are a function of quality

information.

15) Success in life is a function of decision.

16) Life experiences are full of decisions.

17) Decisions change destinies.

18) Never settle for information—always look for revelation.

19) You are where you are today based on your last decision.

20) Information is crucial in decision making.

21) Decision makers rule the world.

22) You can rule your world with quality decisions.

23) As long as you decide rightly, Satan cannot harrass you.

CONDITION TO ANSWERED PRAYERS

REPENTANCE

Repentance is our first step to healing. God will not hear us unless we repent.

Remember...

> *Now we know that God heareth not sinners.*
> **John 9:31**

Genuine repentance is the key to answered prayers.

> *John did baptize in the wilderness,*
> *and preach the baptism of repentance*
> *for the remission of sins.*
> **Mark 1:4**

> *Repent, and be baptized every one of you*
> *in the name of Jesus Christ for the remission of sins,*
> *and ye shall receive the gift of the Holy Ghost.*
> **Acts 2:38**

BE BAPTIZED

We must all be baptized, not only with water, but in the Holy Spirit as well.

Now when all the people were baptized, it came to pass, that Jesus also being baptized, and praying, the heaven was opened, And the Holy Ghost descended in a bodily shape like a dove upon him, and a voice came from heaven, which said, Thou art my beloved Son; in thee I am well pleased.
Luke 3:21-22

Baptism is a condition to answered prayers. *"Be baptized every one of you in the name of Jesus Christ for the remission of sins, and ye shall receive the gift of the Holy Ghost."* (Acts 2:38)

CONFESS OF YOUR SIN
Until we **confess** our sins, **God will not answer our prayers**. *"He that covereth his sins shall not prosper: but whoso confesseth and forsaketh them shall have mercy."* (Proverbs 28:13)
Remember....

Now we know that God heareth not sinners.
John 9:31

It is written, *"If we confess our sins, he is faithful and just to forgive us our sins, and to cleanse us from all unrighteousness."* (1 John 1:7)

ACKNOWLEDGMENT
For all our **prayers** to be answered, we must **acknowledge** the sovereignty of **God and the supremacy**

of Jesus Christ.

In whom we have redemption through his blood, even the forgiveness of sins: Who is the image of the invisible God, the firstborn of every creature: For by him were all things created, that are in heaven, and that are in earth, visible and invisible, whether they be thrones, or dominions, or principalities, or powers: all things were created by him, and for him: And he is before all things, and by him all things consist. And he is the head of the body, the church: who is the beginning, the firstborn from the dead; that in all things he might have the preeminence. For it pleased the Father that in him should all fulness dwell; And, having made peace through the blood of his cross, by him to reconcile all things unto himself; by him, I say, whether they be things in earth, or things in heaven.
Colossians 1:14-20

Acknowledge that we are sinners, that Jesus Christ died for our sins.
Romans 3:23

BORN AGAIN

For **our prayers to be answered, we must be born again**. There are no two ways about it. Recall, *"Neither is there salvation in any other: for there is none other name under heaven given among men, whereby we must be saved."* (Acts 4:12)

*Jesus answered and said unto him, Verily, verily,
I say unto thee, Except a man be born again,
he cannot see the kingdom of God. Nicodemus saith
unto him, How can a man be born when he is old?
can he enter the second time into his mother's womb,
and be born? Jesus answered, Verily, verily, I say unto
thee, Except a man be born of water and of the Spirit, he
cannot enter into the kingdom of God.
That which is born of the flesh is flesh;
and that which is born of the Spirit is spirit.
Marvel not that I said unto thee, Ye must be born again.
The wind bloweth where it listeth, and thou
hearest the sound thereof, but canst not tell
whence it cometh, and whither it goeth:
so is every one that is born of the Spirit.*
JOHN 3:3-8

ASK IN FAITH

It is written, *"But let him ask in faith, nothing wavering. For he that wavereth is like a wave of the sea driven with the wind and tossed. For let not that man think that he shall receive any thing of the Lord. A double minded man is unstable in all his ways."* (James 1:6-8) It takes faith for us to believe that God exists and that He will hear us. Jesus said, *"And all things, whatsoever you shall ask in prayer, believing, you shall receive."* (Matthew 21:22)

WE MUST BE FOCUSED WHEN WE ASK IN FAITH

Every form of distraction is a manipulation of

the devil. Remember, *"The devil came to kill, to steal , and to destroy."* (John 10:10)

And Jesus said unto him, No man,
having put his hand to the plough, and looking back,
is fit for the kingdom of God.
Luke9:62

It takes concentration for our prayers to be **answered by God**.

SUMMARY OF CHAPTER 2

The blood of Jesus Christ is a force of the spirit that cannot be neglected nor ignored by the believer. We are told in the Bible that **the blood of Jesus cleanses us** from all unrightouesness.

*In whom we have redemption through his blood,
even the forgiveness of sins.*
Colissians 1:13

It is also written, *"But if we walk in the light, as he is in the light, we have fellowship one with another, and the blood of Jesus Christ his Son cleanseth us from all sin."* (1 John 1:7)

In conclusion, we must therefore do the following:

—We must apply the blood of Jesus appropriately.

—The blood of Jesus is our last weapon against the devil.

—We must repent of our sins.

—We must observe all the conditions for answered prayers.

CHAPTER 3
THE BENEFITS OF THE BLOOD OF JESUS

But if we walk in the light, as he is in the light, we have fellowship one with another, and the blood of Jesus Christ his Son cleanseth us from all sin.
1 John 1:7

THE BLOOD OF JESUS CHRIST IS OUR VICTORY TICKET IN PRAYERS

Although when we plead the blood of Jesus, we literally utter words out of our mouth. The mystery behind the **blood of Jesus Christ** that makes it strange is that the **blood speaks**.

And to Jesus the mediator of the new covenant, and to the blood of sprinkling, that speaketh better things than that of Abel.
Hebrews 12:24

Every time the **blood speaks before the Father,** it vindicates us from **condemnation and punishment**. It **validates and confirms** our **prayer petition** and renders **judgment** to the offender—the wicked devil.

CAIN AND ABEL EXAMPLE FROM GENESIS

And he said, What hast thou done? the voice of thy brother's blood crieth unto me from the ground. And now art thou cursed from the earth, which hath opened her mouth to receive thy brother's blood from thy hand; When thou tillest the ground, it shall not henceforth yield unto thee her strength; a fugitive and a vagabond shalt thou be in the earth.
Genesis 4:10-12

THE BLOOD OF JESUS CHRIST NEUTRALIZES EVERY SPELL AND CURSE AGAINST US

And he said, That which cometh out of the man, that defileth the man. For from within, out of the heart of men, proceed evil thoughts, adulteries, fornications, murders, Thefts, covetousness, wickedness, deceit, lasciviousness, an evil eye, blasphemy, pride, foolishness: All these evil things come from within, and defile the man.
Mark 7:20-23

All curses, spells and evil attacks come from the heart. It is always generated from the conscience. The **blood of Jesus Christ** purges our conscience from all dead works.

*How much more shall the blood of Christ,
who through the eternal Spirit offered himself without
spot to God, purge your conscience from dead works to
serve the living God?*
Hebrews 9:14

THE BLOOD OF JESUS
DELIVERS US FROM DEPRESSION

As long as you can appropriate the **blood of Jesus Christ, we will not suffer depression in our life time**. *"Neither be ye sorry; for the joy of the Lord is your strength."* (Nehemiah 8:10) As long as we genuinely look up to Jesus and appropriate the blood of Jesus, **the devil has no chance**. *"Neither give place to the devil."* (Ephesians 4:27)

THE BLOOD OF JESUS
HEALS OUR BODY, SOUL & SPIRIT

"After the same manner also he took the cup, when he had supped, saying, this cup is the new testament in my blood: this do ye, as oft as ye drink it, in remembrance of me." (1 Corinthians 11:25) Every time we take the communion, we eat **the blood of Jesus**. This **blood** heals, delivers, protects and rejuvenates our soul body and spirit.

THE BLOOD OF JESUS GURANTEES US EXTRA STRENGTH

Remember…

Man did eat angels' food: he sent them meat to the full.
Psalms 78:25

WHEN ELIJAH ATE THIS WHAT HAPPENED TO HIM?

The Bible recorded that when Elijah ate this food, he was strengthened for 40 days and 40 nights. "And he arose, and did eat and drink, and went in the strength of that meat forty days and forty nights unto Horeb the mount of God." (1 Kings 19:8)

The blood of Jesus therefore guarantees extra strength.

THE BLOOD OPENS OUR UNDERSTANDING TO THE MYSTERIES OF GOD

As long as we take the **blood of Jesus** in faith, it **illuminates and enlightens** our understanding. *"Then opened he their understanding, that they might understand the scriptures."* (Luke 24:45)

"And it came to pass, as he sat at meat with them, he took bread, and blessed it, and brake, and gave to them. And their eyes were opened, and they knew him; and he vanished out of their sight." (Luke 24:30-31)

SUMMARY OF CHAPTER 3

—Always apply the blood of Jesus in faith.

—Never mock with the mysteries of the blood of Jeus Christ.

—Always plead the blood of Jesus Christ in prayers.

—Take advantage of all the benefits of the blood of Jesus.

—The blood is our last weapon against the adversary.

—Always use the blood as a shield for your defense.

—Always confess the blood of Jesus for the remission of sins.

—Engage the mystery of the blood for breakthrough.

—Engage the mystery of the blood for deliverance.

—Engage the mystery of the blood for protection.

Remember...

FEAR EQUALS:

F—FALSE

E— — EVIDENCE

A— — — APPEARING

R— — — — REAL

Remember...

FAIL MEANS:

F—FIRST

A— — ATTEMPT

I— — — IN

L— — — — LEARNING

God works with your faith in the blood of Jesus, while the devil attacks us with fear. A ritual practice of pleading the blood of Jesus Christ drives away the devil.

PRAYER POINTS TO OVERCOME
TRIALS BY THE HELP OF THE HOLY SPIRIT

1) Father Lord, deliver me from this present trial, in the name of Jesus.

2) Almighty Father, break me out of this present obscurity, in the name of Jesus.

3) Holy Spirit, help me to overcome this trial, in Jesus name.

4) Holy Spirit, speak to me, in the name of Jesus.

5) Holy Spirit, minister to my subconscious spirit, in the name of Jesus.

6) Fire of God, burn down every mountain of difficulty, in the name of Jesus.

7) Holy Ghost, baptize me with your fire, in the name of Jesus.

8) Holy Spirit, go before me and favor me in this present challenge, in the name of Jesus.

9) Spirit of God, grant me liberty and freedom by the fire of the Holy Spirit, in the name of Jesus.

10) Father Lord, intervene on my behalf, in the name of Jesus.

11) Ancient of day, liberate me this season, in the name

of Jesus.

12) Immortal redeemer, bring me higher above these prevailing changes.

13) Lord God, turn this present obstacale into my miracle, in the name of Jesus.

14) Fire of God, break down these obstacles for me, in the name of Jesus.

15) Holy Spirit, favor me in, Jesus name.

16) Holy Spirit. release me from this challenge, in the name of Jesus.

17) Holy Spirit, become my compionion, in Jesus name.

18) Holy Spirit, represent me in this matter.

19) Holy Spirit, elevant me beyond my own immagination, in the name of Jesus.

20) Holy Spirit, do not allow my enemies to truimph over my life, in the name of Jesus.

21) Fire of God, protect me, in the name of Jesus.

22) Fire of God, destroy my enemies, in the name of Jesus.

23) Fire of God, build a wall around me, in the name of Jesus.

24) Fire of God, expose my enemies, in the name of Jesus.

25) Fire of God, prove yourself, in the name of Jesus.

26) Holy Spirit, represent me in jesus name.

27) Holy Spirit, release your boldnes into my life.

28) Holy Spirit, grant me signs and wonders.

29) Holy Spirit, make me a living wonder in my lifetime.

30) Holy Spirit, turn my life around, in the name of Jesus.

31) Holy Spirit, I will not remain at this level, in the name of Jesus.

32) Spirit of God, lift me higher, in the mighty name of Jesus.

33) Angels of God, minister unto me, in the name of Jesus.

34) Hand of God, separate me this season, in the name of Jesus.

SUMMARY

*Much more then, being now justified by his blood,
we shall be saved from wrath through him.*
Romans 5:9

*And they overcame him by the blood of the Lamb,
and by the word of their testimony;
and they loved not their lives unto the death.*
Revelation 12:11

The blood of Jesus is our weapon of war. We must therefore engage the enemy with the blood of Jesus as our counter offensive weapon. Every time we plead the blood of jesus christ, the enemy—Satan—retreats.

*Christ hath redeemed us from the curse of the law, being
made a curse for us: for it is written, Cursed is every one
that hangeth on a tree: That the blessing of Abraham
might come on the Gentiles through Jesus Christ; that
we might receive the promise of the Spirit through faith.*
Galatians 3:13-14

I admonish you in the lord, do not take the shedding blood of Jesus for granted. We must appropriate the blood of Jesus accordingly.

Purge out therefore the old leaven, that ye may be a new lump, as ye are unleavened. For even Christ our passover is sacrificed for us.
1 Corinthians 5:7

We must take advantage of the blood of Jesus Christ.

CONCLUSION

And there are three that bear witness in earth, the Spirit, and the water, and the blood: and these three agree in one.
1 John 5:8

The **blood of Jesus** is our last weapon to pull the trigger against Satan (the devil). As a **spiritual law enforcement officer** with the accreditation of the **blood of Jesus** and a **warrant for the arrest** of the devil, we must engage the **blood of jesus appropriately**. As you finish reading this book, make it your ritual practice to **plead the blood of Jesus daily in prayers**.

And they overcame him by the blood of the Lamb, and by the word of their testimony; and they loved not their lives unto the death.
Revelation 12:11

We must constantly plead the **blood of Jesus in prayers** against all challenges and counterattacks of the **devil**. In my understanding, as long as we **plead the blood of jesus**, we are sure to **prevail** against our adversary—the devil

> *For the life of the flesh is in the blood.*
> **Leviticus 17:11**

But we cannot plead the blood appropriately if we have not given our lives to Jesus Christ.
Recall…

And almost all things are by the law purged with blood; and without shedding of blood is no remission.
Hebrews 9:22

Remember….

Now we know that God heareth not sinners: but if any man be a worshipper of God, and doeth his will, him he heareth
John 9:31

But if we walk in the light, as he is in the light, we have fellowship one with another, and the blood of Jesus Christ his Son cleanseth us from all sin.
1 John 1:7

"We must be born again"

*Therefore if any man be in Christ, he is a new creature:
old things are passed away;
behold, all things are become new.*
2 Corinthians 5:17

Now repeat this prayer after me:

Say Lord Jesus, I accept you today, as my Lord and my savior. Forgive me of my sins, wash me with your blood. Right now, I believe I am sanctified, I am saved, I am free. I am free from the power of sin, to serve the Lord Jesus. Thank you Lord for saving me. Amen.

Congratulations. You are now...

...a BORN AGAIN CHRISTIAN.

Again I say to you—CONGRATULATIONS!

What must I do to determine my divine visitation?

To determine divine visitation you must be born again! The word says as many as received him, to them gave He power to become the sons of God. Even to them that believe on his name.

To qualify for divine visitation, do the following sincerely:

1) Acknowledge that you are a sinner and that He

died for you. (Romans 3:23)

2) Repent of your sins. (Acts 3:19, Luke 13:5, 2 Peter 3:9)

3) Believe in your heart that Jesus died for your sin. (Romans 10:10)

4) Confess Jesus as the Lord over your life. (Romans 10:10, Acts 2:21)

NOW REPEAT THIS PRAYER AFTER ME:
Say Lord Jesus, I accept you today, as my Lord and my savior, forgive me of my sins wash me with your blood. Right now, I believe, I am sanctified, I am save, I am free, I am free from the Power of sin to serve the Lord Jesus. Thank you Lord for saving me. Amen.

Congratulations.

YOU ARE NOW A BORN AGAIN CHRISTAIN!

Again, I say to you—congratulations!

I adjure you to watch the Spirit of God bear witness with your Spirit confirming His word with signs following. The word says the Spirit itself beareth witness with our spirit, that we are the children of God. Join a bible believing church or join us on our weekly and Sunday worship services at 343 Sanford Avenue Newark New Jersey 07106.

WISDOM KEYS

— Every productive society is a society heading to the top.

— Millions of Nigerians run away from Nigeria. Very few Nigerians stay in Nigeria.

— My decision to return Nigeria is the will of God for my life.

— My shortcoming in America after 18 years is the fact that I've trained me to be wise, to think, reflect and reason appropriately.

— If you train your mind to reason, it will train your hands to earn money.

— It is absurd to use the money of the heathen to build the kingdom of the living God.

— Every ministry reveals its agenda and VISION either at the beginning or at the end.

— Be careful of your life. It is your first ministry.

— The average American mind is conditioned for a continual quest to get new things and discard the old.

—When I considered well, my BMW jeep became my initial deposit for the work of the ministry in Nigeria.

—Money will never fall from any tree or person. Make up your mind to be independent today.

—Everyone is waiting for you to change your mind. Until you change your thinking, nothing changes around you.

—Multiple academic degrees in other disciplines gave me the chance to think and reason.

—Whatever anyone is thinking at any time reveals what is inside of their heart.

—All planned events are the product of meditation.

—Every event is designed for a designated timeline.

—Wisdom is your ability to think, to create and invent.

— If you can think wisely enough, you will come out of debt.

—The distance between you and your success is your innovative and creative ability to think well.

—Success is the result of hard work, commitment, resolve and determined learning from past mistakes and failings.

—If you organize your mind, you have organized your life and destiny.

—There is a thin line between success and failure.

—Wealth is your ability to think, power is your ability to reason and success is your ability to be informed.

—If you can make use of your mind by thinking and reasoning, God will make use of your life and destiny.

—Reflect, reason, think and be Great.

—Famous people are born of woman.

—That you will make it is your intention, that you will survive is your resolve, that you will succeed with changes is your determination, personal efforts and hard work.

—No man was born a failure.

—Lack of vision is the result of failure.

—Working with mental patients encourages and aspire me to be a productive observant and dedicated to my assignment.

—Successful people are not magicians. It is the will-power, combined with hard work and determination and a resolve to succeed, that make them succeed.

—In the unequivocal state of the mind, intention is not a location or a position. It is the state of the mind.

—So many people think that they think.

—The mind is used to think, to reflect and to reason.

—You will remain blind with your eyes open until you can see with your mind by thinking.

—There is no favoritism in accurate and precise calculation.

—Although knowledge is power, information is the key and gateway to a great future.

—It will take the hand of God to move the hand of man.

—With the backing of the great wise God, nothing will disconnect you from your inheritance.

—As long as you have wisdom and understanding of God, Satan and evil cannot manipulate your life and destiny.

—You have come this far in life by your own judgment and the decisions you made in the past. Now lean in and listen to God for another dimension of greatness.

—Great people are ordinary people. It is extra ordinary efforts and the price of sacrifice that produces greatness in them.

—As a mental direct care worker, I saw a great pastor and a motivational speaker within myself.

—A menial job does not reduce your self-worth. Until you resolve to achieve greatness and see greatness in all you do, you will never count in your community.

—The principle of Jesus will solve your gambling and addiction problems.

—The man of Jesus will lead you into heaven.

—Everyone has their self-appraisal and what they think about you. Until you discover yourself, other opinions about you will alter the real you.

—Supervisors and directors are just a position in the chain of command in a workplace. Never allow your supervisor hierarchy to alter your opinion of yourself.

—Everyone can come out of debt if they make up their mind.

—The fact that I am not a decision-maker at work does not diminish my contribution to my world.

—Although it appears like it was a poor decision to accept a direct care employment at a psychiatric hospital, as I reflect on my nine years of that experience, it became apparent that I have learned and experienced enough for my next assignment.

—Self-encouragement and determination is a resolve of the heart.

—If you are determined to make a difference and do the things that make a difference, you will eventually make a difference.

—Good things do not come easy.

—Short cuts will cut your life short.

—Those who look ahead move ahead.

—Life is all about making an impact. In your lifetime strive to make an impact in your community.

—Make friends and connect with people who are moving ahead of you in life.

—If you can look around well, you have come a long way in your life, made a lot of difference and realized a lot of success in life.

—If you are my old friend, hurry up to reach out to me before I become a stranger to you.

—I am blessed with inspirations from God that changed my interpretation of the world around me.

—I thought I was stagnant and lonely until I looked around and noticed my children running around and my wife cooking.

— At 40, I resigned my job to seek the Lord forever.

—My ministry took a drastic rise to the top when the wisdom of God visited me with knowledge and understanding.

—You will be a better person if you understand the characteristics of your personality like your mood swings, attitudes and habits.

—It is the seed of love you sow into the heart of a child and a woman that you reap in due time.

—Love is not selfish. Love shares everything, including the concealed secrets of the mind.

—As long as you have a prayer life and a Bible, you will never feel lonely in the race of life.

—When good friends disconnect from you, let them go. They might have seen something new in a different direction.

—Confidence in yourself and in God is the only way to bring you out of captivity

—Never train a child to waste his or her time.

—The mind is the greatest asset of a great future.

—You walk by common sense, run by principles and fly by instruction.

—Those who become successful in life did it by self-determination, hard work and learning from past failures.

—Most successful people are lonely people. No one renders help to them, believing they are already successful. Except when they seek for more knowledge and information, they are all alone.

— I have seen a towing truck vehicle. I have also seen a towing ship in the water. But I have never seen a towing airplane in the air.

—I exercise my judgment and make a decision every minute of the day. Decisions are crucial, critical and vital with reference to your future.

—So many people wish for a great future. You can only work towards a great future.

—Your celebrity status began when you discovered your talent. What are you good at? Work at it with all your commitment.

—Prayers will sustain you, but the wisdom of God will prosper you.

—When I met Oyedepo, his teachings changed my perspective. But when I met Ibiyeomie, his teachings changed my perception.

— I will be successful in ministry if only I concentrate and focus my energy in the work of the ministry.

— It took the late Dr. Norman Vincent Peale's book to open my mind towards the kingdom of success.

CHAPTER 4
PRAYER OF SALVATION

I am glad you have read this book all the way from the beginning to this point. All I have said from the beginning will remain a mystery until you commit it into practice.

And before you do so, I want you—if you have not given your life to Jesus already—to do so now. Give your life to Christ. I want you to know the truth! The truth is that Jesus died for your sins and because He died, you must be alive and prosperous.

What must I do to truly experiene genuine **SALVATION**?

To determine divine visitation, you must be born again! The word says, *"As many as received Him, to them gave He power to become the sons of God. Even to them that believe on his name."* (John 1:12)

To qualify for **divine visitation**, do the following with sincerity—

1) Acknowledge that you are a sinner and that He died for you. (Romans 3:23)
2) Repent of your sins. (Acts 3:19, Luke 13:5, 2 Peter 3:9)
3) Believe in your heart that Jesus died for your sins. (Romans 10:10)

4) Confess Jesus as the Lord over your life. (Romans 10:10, Acts 2:21)

Now repeat this prayer after me:

Say Lord Jesus, I accept you today, as my Lord and my savior. Forgive me of my sins, wash me with your blood. Right now, I believe I am sanctified, I am saved, I am free. I am free from the power of sin, to serve the Lord Jesus. Thank you Lord for saving me. Amen.

Congratulations. You are now...

A BORN AGAIN CHRISTIAN.

Again I say to you—CONGRATULATIONS!

I adjure you to watch the Spirit of God bear witness with your Spirit, confirming His word with subsequent signs. The word says, *"The Spirit itself beareth witness with our spirit, that we are the children of God."* (Romans 8:16)

Chapter 4   Prayer of Salvation

MIRACLE CARE OUTREACH

*"...But that the members should have
the same care one for another"*
1 Corinthians 12:25

We are all members of the body of Christ. Jesus commanded us to love our neighbor as ourselves. This includes caring for one another as a member of one body. True love is expressed in caring and giving. The word says, for God so Love He gave....

Reach out to someone in need of Jesus. Help someone in crisis find Christ. Look out and prove your love to Jesus by caring and inviting your friends and associates to find Jesus the Healer.

Invite your friends to our Home Care Cell Fellowship (Miracle Chapel Intl. Satellite Fellowship). We're in the U.S. at 33 Schley Street, Newark, New Jersey 07112. Home Care Cell Fellowship Group meets every Tuesday at 6:00pm-7:00pm.

If you are in Nigeria—MIRACLE OF GOD MINISTRIES, aka "MIRACLE CHAPEL INTL." Mpama–Egbu-Owerri Imo state Nigeria.

LIFE IS NOT ALL ABOUT DURATION, BUT IT'S ALL ABOUT DONATION

What does this statement mean?
Life consists not in accumulation of material

wealth. (Luke 12:15) But it's all about liberality…i.e., what you can give and share with others. (Proverbs 11:25) When you live for others, you live forever—because you outlive your generation by the legacy you leave behind after you depart into glory to be with the Lord. But when you live for yourself, when you are reduced to SELF—you are easily forgotten when you die and depart in glory.

Permit me to admonish you today to live your life to be a blessing to a soul connected to you today. I want you to know that so many souls are connected and looking up to you, and through you so many souls will be saved and rescued from destruction. Will you disciple someone today to find Jesus Christ?

As a genuine Christian, it is your duty to evangelize Jesus Christ to all you meet on your way. Jesus is still in the healing business—Jesus is still doing miracles, from time of old to now. Therefore, tell someone about Jesus Christ today, disciple and bring them to Church. *Philip findeth Nathanael…* (John 1:45)

Please prove the sincerity of your love for God today, please become a soul winner. The dignity of your Christianity is hidden in your boldness to proclaim and evangelize Jesus Christ to all you meet on your way. There is a question mark on the integrity of your Christianity until you become a life soul winner. Invite someone to join us worship the Lord Jesus this coming Sunday. Amen.

MIRACLE OF GOD MINISTRIES
PILLARS OF THE COMMISSION

We Believe, Preach and Practice the following:

1) We believe and preach Salvation to every living human being.

2) We believe and preach Repentance and Forgiveness of sins.

3) We believe and preach the baptism of the Holy Spirit and Spiritual gifts.

4) We believe and teach Prosperity.

5) We believe and preach Divine Healing and Miracles—Signs and Wonder.

6) We believe and preach Faith.

7) We believe and proclaim the Power of God (Supernatural).

8) We believe and proclaim Praise and Worship to God.

9) We believe and preach Wisdom.

10) We believe and preach Holiness (Consecration).

11) We believe and preach Vision.

12) We believe and teach the Word of God.

13) We believe and teach Success.

14) We believe and practice Prayer.

15) We believe and teach Deliverance.

These 15 stones form the Pillars of Our Commission. Become part of this church family and follow this great move of God.

MY HEARTFELT PRAYER FOR YOU

It is my burning desire for God to touch you through one of our teaching books or CDs. It also my personal desire for you encounter God for yourself.

Now let me Pray for you:

I plead the precious blood of Jesus over your life. I decree and declare that no weapon fashioned against you shall ever prosper, every tongue that shall rise up against you God shall condemn it in judgement. From this day I declare your name in the lamb book of life. From this great day I declare goodness and mercy to hunt you down all the days of your life. Remain blessed, in Jesus name. Amen.

TIME TO TURN TO GOD

WHAT SHALL A MAN GIVE IN EXCHAENGE FOR HIS SOUL?

For what shall it profit a man, if he shall gain the whole world, and lose his own soul? Or what shall a man give in exchange for his soul?
Mark 8:36-37

ETERNITY IS REAL, HEAVEN IS SURE, BUT HELL IS INEVITABLE

We must make plans and be prepared to make heaven at last. Have you ever wondered about what will happened to your soul when you die? It is not a frightening question? We must answer this question while we are yet alive. We must live a righteous lifestyle for the master, Jesus Christ. We must **love** our friends and neighbor as ourselves. We must obey the 10 commandment—especially the greatest commandment. *"Jesus said unto him, Thou shalt love the Lord thy God with all thy heart, and with all thy soul, and with all thy mind. This is the first and great commandment. And the second is like unto it, Thou shalt love thy neighbour as thyself."* (Matthew 22:37-39)

ABOUT THE AUTHOR

Rev. Franklin N. Abazie is the founding and Presiding Pastor of Miracle of God Ministries, with headquarters in Newark, New Jersey USA and a branch church in Owerri-Imo State Nigeria. He is following the footsteps of one of his mentors, the healing evangelist Oral Roberts of the blessed memory. The Lord passed Oral Roberts' healing mantle two days before he went to be with the Lord at age 91 into the hands of healing evangelist Rev. Franklin N. Abazie in a vision.

In all his services, the Power and Presence of God is present to heal all in his audience. Rev. Abazie is an ordained man of God, with a Healing Ministry reviving the healing and miracle ministry of Jesus Christ of Nazareth.

Pastor Franklin N. Abazie, has been called by God with a unique mandate: **"THE MOMENT IS DUE TO IMPACT YOUR WORLD THROUGH THE REVIVAL OF THE HEALING AND MIRACLE MINISTRY OF JESUS CHRIST OF NAZARETH.**

"I AM SENDING YOU TO RESTORE HEALTH UNTO THEE AND I WILL HEAL THEE OF THY WOUNDS, SAID THE LORD OF HOST."

Chapter 5   About the Author

Rev. Abazie is a gifted, ardent teacher of the word of God, who operates also in the office of a Prophet, generating and attracting undeniable signs and wonders, special miracles and healings, with apostolic fireworks of the Holy Ghost. He is the founding and presiding senior Pastor of this fast growing Healing Ministry. He has written over 86 inspirational, healing and transforming books covering almost all aspects of divine healing and life. He is happily married and blessed with children.

BOOKS BY REV. FRANKLIN N. ABAZIE:

1) The Outcome of Faith
2) Understanding the Secret of Prevailing Prayers
3) Commanding Abundance
4) Understanding the Secret of the Man God Uses
5) Activating My Due Season
6) Overcoming Divine Verdicts
7) The Outcome of Divine Wisdom
8) Understanding God's Restoration Mandate
9) Walking In the Victory and Authority of the Truth
10) God's Covenant Exemption
11) Destiny Restoration Pillars
12) Provoking Acceptable Praise
13) Understanding Divine Judgment
14) Activating Angelic Re-enforcement
15) Provoking Un-Merited Favo
16) The Benefits of the Speaking Faith
17) Understanding Divine Arrangement
18) How to Keep Your Healing
19) Understanding the Mysteries of the Speaking Faith
20) Understanding the Mysteries of Prophetic Healing
21) Operating Under the Rules of Creative Healing
22) Understanding the Joy of Breakthrough
23) Understanding the Mystery of Breakthrough
24) Understanding Divine Prosperity
25) Understanding Divine Healing
26) Retaining Your Inheritance
27) Overcoming Confusing Spirit
28) Commanding Angelic Escorts

29) Enforcing Your Inheritance In Christ Jesus
30) Understanding Your Guardian Angels
31) Overcoming the Dominion of Sin
32) Understanding the Voice of God
33) The Outstanding Benefits of the Anointing
34) The Audacity of the Blood of Jesus
35) Walking in the Reality of the Anointing
36) Escaping the Nightmare of Poverty
37) Understanding Your Harvest Season
38) Activating Your Success Buttons
39) Overcoming the Forces of Darkness
40) Overcoming the Devices of the Devil
41) Overcoming Demonic Agents
42) Overcoming the Sorrows of Failure
43) Rejecting the Sorrows of Failure
44) Resisting the Sorrows of Poverty
45) Restoring Broken Marriages
46) Redeeming Your Days
47) The Force of Vision
48) Overcoming the Forces of Ignorance
49) Understanding the Sacrifice of Small Beginning
50) The Might of Small Beginning
51) Understanding the Mysteries of Prophesy
52) Overcoming Dream Nightmares
53) Breaking the Shackles of the Curse of the Law
54) Understanding the Joy of Harvest
55) Wisdom for Signs & Wonders
56) Wisdom for Generational Impact
57) Wisdom for Marriage Stability
58) Understanding the Number of Your Days

59) Enforcing Your Kingdom Rights
60) Escaping the Traps of Immoralities
61) Escaping the Trap of Poverty
62) Accessing Biblical Prosperity
63) Accessing True Riches in Christ
64) Silencing the Voice of the Accuser
65) Overcoming the Forces of Oppositions
66) Quenching the Voice of the Avenger
67) Silencing Demonic Prediction & Projection
68) Silencing Your Mocker
69) Understanding the Power of the Holy Ghost
70) Understanding the Baptism of Power
71) The Mystery of the Blood of Jesus
72) Understanding the Mystery of Sanctification
73) Understanding the Power of Holiness
74) Understanding the Forces of Purity & Righteousness
75) Activating the Forces of Vengeance
76) Appreciating the Mystery of Restoration
77) Overcoming the Projection & Prediction of the Enemy
78) Engaging the Mystery of the Blood
79) Commanding the Power of the Speaking Faith
80) Uprooting the Forces Against Your Rising
81) Overcoming Mere Success Syndrome
82) Understanding Divine Sentence
83) Understanding the Mystery of Praise
84) Understanding the Author of Faith
85) The Mystery of the Finisher of Faith
86) Attracting Supernatural Favor

MIRACLE OF GOD MINISTRIES

NIGERIA CRUSADE   2012

MIRACLE OF GOD MINISTRIES
NIGERIA CRUSADE
2012

MIRACLE OF GOD MINISTRIES
NIGERIA CRUSADE 2012

MIRACLE OF GOD MINISTRIES

NIGERIA CRUSADE

2012

MIRACLE OF GOD MINISTRIES

NIGERIA CRUSADE

2012

www.ingramcontent.com/pod-product-compliance
Lightning Source LLC
Chambersburg PA
CBHW020035120526
44588CB00031B/707